Higher Learning in the Nation's Service

A CARNEGIE FOUNDATION ESSAY

HIGHER LEARNING IN THE NATION'S SERVICE

ERNEST L. BOYER & FRED M. HECHINGER

THE CARNEGIE FOUNDATION FOR THE
ADVANCEMENT OF TEACHING

1785 Massachusetts Avenue, N.W.
Washington, D.C. 20036

Copies are available from The Carnegie Foundation for the
Advancement of Teaching, 1785 Massachusetts Avenue, N.W.,
Washington, D.C. 20036.

ISBN 0-931050-20-0

LC 81-70738

Designed by Julian Waters, Bookmark Studio

Manufactured in the United States
of America

CONTENTS

PREFACE

THIS ESSAY is one in a series in which The Carnegie Foundation for the Advancement of Teaching seeks to stimulate thought and discussion about the aims of education. In this report, *Higher Learning in the Nation's Service,* we intentionally have chosen a huge canvas, have used broad strokes to picture the current condition of higher learning in America, and have sketched proposals for the future. In subsequent essays we plan to look more closely at specific topics and set forth in more detail recommendations relating to both the purposes and the content of higher education.

At the outset, we underscore the obvious point that there are more than 3,000 colleges and universities in America with different traditions, and, frequently, with different missions. We applaud the richness of this diversity and believe strongly that it should be strengthened, not eroded. We also believe, however, that there are essential overarching missions that concern the enterprise of higher learning overall. It is to these larger concerns that this essay is addressed.

At first glance, our title may seem presumptuous in linking "higher learning" and "the nation's service." From one perspective, American colleges and universities have little to do with larger social goals. They are concerned with the work of individual scholars and with educating individual students. Yet, many times throughout our history, profound questions of national purpose have become intertwined with higher learning's traditional functions of teaching and research. From the very first, the nation's colleges and universities have been considered "useful" not only to individual students but also to the larger community that granted them recognition and support.

In focusing on higher learning and the nation, we clearly identify ourselves with those who take at least qualified pride in what colleges and universities have accomplished. But this record, remarkable as it is, also poses crucial questions for academic leaders in the 1980s. To what extent, if any, can—or should—a college or university today and in the coming decades attempt to define purposes and goals distinct from those of the nation as a whole? If one were to peel away all of the layers of purpose "imposed" on higher education by society, what would be left that an institution could claim as unmistakably its own?

This is a particularly timely moment to consider these essential questions. After decades of phenomenal success, American higher education is puzzled and unsure. Having long been in the center of the national arena, it finds itself on the sidelines. It is hardly surprising that, under such conditions, higher learning is confused about its purposes and goals.

In this essay, therefore, we do not intend merely to recount or celebrate higher learning's past service to the nation, important as that may have been. Our primary purpose is to urge colleges and universities to use the current period of transition to rediscover how their own unique historic purposes can serve the nation's interests in new and vital ways. To achieve this, we focus especially on four goals we believe to be centrally important.

First, we call upon higher learning to renew its commitment to teach a new generation of students that differs from those served in the past. Second, we argue that the nation's interest will require a vigorous program of independent university-based research with appropriate linkages to other laboratories and research institutes. Third, as a new approach to public service, we advocate public policy studies for all students, especially encouraging a new program of civic education for adults.

Finally, as a capstone, we urge colleges and universities to maintain their independence and help students to use knowledge wisely so that higher education's dual role of servant and critic of society may be vigorously protected and advanced. As higher learning gives new meaning to its historic purposes of teaching, research, and public service, the future of both the academy and the nation will be made more secure.

ERNEST L. BOYER

Washington, D.C.   FRED M. HECHINGER

Section One

PERSPECTIVES

I

THE LOSS OF CONFIDENCE

HIGHER EDUCATION IN AMERICA is suffering from a loss of overall direction, a nagging feeling that it is no longer at the vital center of the nation's work. After decades of enthusiastic growth, many colleges now face confusion over goals, reduced support, and an uncertain future.

This loss of confidence reflects, at least in part, our larger confusion as a nation. In America today there are few deeply held commitments on which we can agree and few sharply defined goals that guide our course. As a nation, we are confused about our role in the world and about priorities at home. We are shaken by a growing awareness of new limits—of resources that once were thought unlimited, of growth that once was thought unending, and of economic and political power that once was considered exclusively our own.

For the first time in nearly half a century, America's colleges and universities are not collectively caught up in some urgent national endeavor. Academic specialists who, in the heyday of the postwar boom, were called upon to help solve every manner of social and economic problem, feel bypassed as calls from Washington come less frequently than before. Today, campuses are not being called upon to win a global war or build Quonset huts for returning veterans. They are not trying to beat the Russians to the moon, or gearing up to implement new programs, as in the heady days of the New Deal, the New Frontier, and the Great Society. Today, higher education appears to be adrift because, in some respects, the nation is adrift.

The malaise on campus also reflects higher education's rapid shift from expansion to constraint, the spread of regulations, and procedures that seem to undermine the creative process. Today many educators are preoccupied with the politics and management of education. When administrators are forced to spend countless hours on logistics, litigation, and budget balancing, the prospects for imagining are diminished and the vitality of the institution is diminished, too. A sense of powerlessness sets in, and higher learning becomes just another regulated industry.

Without judging the underlying merit of government regulations, one cannot avoid the fact that, cumulatively, time-consuming mandates have altered the climate of higher education. Each new demand means that priorities must be shifted. Overplanning and overreporting restrict the freedom that is necessary for creative thought. Time consumed is potential lost.

In such a climate, there are pessimists who question whether even small academic gains can be made today. They embrace the dark sentiments of the poet-turned-critic, Matthew Arnold, who wrote in 1863 that in some epochs, creativity is simply not possible. In such times, Arnold said, all one can manage is a "poor, starved, fragmentary, inadequate creation."[1]

The declining influence of the professoriate also accounts for anxiety on campus. In the 1950s and early 1960s, professors were in the driver's seat. Deans and department chairmen bid against each other for every gifted graduate student and young scholar. The more desirable the candidate, the more generous the offer. Laboratory lights burned late into the night. Government grants and contracts generously supported the great research universities of the nation. Faculty stars jetted between the campus, corporate headquarters, and the nation's capital.

That glittering age of academic power and prestige was badly tarnished in the 1960s. Protesting students charged, with considerable reason, that, amid the abundance of research and the euphoria of growth, they had been forgotten. As campuses grew into giant multiversities, students began to carry placards proclaiming: "I am a human being. Do not fold, spindle, or mutilate." Critical students viewed the university as another tool of "the Establishment" that turned them into cogs of a great impersonal machine. They demanded both more attention and fewer regulations.

As the war in Vietnam escalated, student protesters accused campuses of complicity with the so-called military industrial complex, and frequently they found strong allies among their teachers. Many professors also criticized the country's direction—the slow pace at which the disenfranchised were gaining civil rights, the nation's disastrous course in Indochina, the growing power of giant institutions.

Faculties were less sympathetic when students complained about campus rules and regulations; however, it seemed prudent to many deans and curriculum committees to buy peace—by yielding to the "nonnegotiable demands." Accordingly, course requirements were eased or dropped, grades were deemphasized or inflated, and rules of student conduct were modified or abolished. This pattern was not universal, to be sure, but campus confrontations were sufficiently widespread to cause many Americans to view the whole affair with profound disapproval and open disgust.

Higher education's prestige quickly declined as the era of great expansion ended. While the nation's unsolved problems—economic, technological, social, diplomatic, and environmental—were as acute as ever, government decision-makers seemed less and less inclined to turn to the campuses for help. Increasingly, the nation's managers sought advice, not from scholars, but from pollsters and special interest groups.

The impact of this shift in strategy was painfully illustrated when President Carter called an array of influential persons and advocates of special interests to Camp David for consultations that were billed as the prelude to dramatic shifts in public policy. But what began as a "summit conference" in search of a national purpose ended as a Babel of diverse opinions reflecting a plethora of constituencies jockeying for position.

It would be misleading to place all—or even most—of the blame for higher education's loss of confidence on the shoulders of the colleges and universities themselves. They can hardly be blamed for the larger confusions of the nation; for the demographic shifts that may seriously affect enrollments; or for inflation, high interest rates, or the slowdown in economic productivity that have put campuses in such a painful economic squeeze.

Still, it must be candidly acknowledged that higher education itself, like much of the rest of society, seems to have lost confidence in its own purposes and goals. Absent a larger vision, some campuses have become consumer-driven enterprises, following the marketplace, constantly juggling goals and programs to new demands. When, for example, students asked for more job training, some colleges with no tradition in career education rushed to add new courses. In the process, they duplicated the work of other institutions and paid little attention to the need for a strong and durable vision of their own.

Higher education does have an obligation to respond to student needs and preparing students for vocation is, of course, essential. After all, it was the *neglect* of these interests in the days of the great expansion that alienated students. But there is a crucial difference between thoughtfully responding to new demands in the context of clearly defined goals and randomly starting programs unrelated to the colleges' own objectives. The first discharges a basic responsibility of the institution to serve students; the second abandons an equally basic responsibility to match programs and objectives.

Lacking vision and inspiration, America's colleges and

universities seem today to be waiting for new cues from off-stage prompters rather than setting their own objectives. Another Sputnik, or its equivalent, might spark renewed interest in education and fuel a drive for more research. A new wave of campus unrest would once again put higher education in the spotlight. Something equivalent to a new G.I. Bill would surely revitalize the campus. But any such event, even if it should come, would only mask the central problem that now confronts us: the apparent inability of higher learning to clarify *its own* mission and define *for itself* the role it best can play in our nation's future.

Threatened by declining enrollments, suffocating regulations, and reduced support, campuses are forced to fight for budgets and scramble to recruit students. Little time is left to consider what it means to be an educated person. Little attention is paid to that essential antidote to intellectual and social chaos—a sense of purpose without which no institution, community, or nation can survive. Necessary under any circumstances, such a common vision is particularly crucial when a flood of undigested information comes cascading down on a society rendered all the more complex by experts who barely understand each other.

We believe campuses must become something more than academic supermarkets. As enrollments shrink, colleges may, in desperation, give students anything they want, with a minimum of effort and with no clearly defined core of demanding studies. This strategy—already being followed by a small but worrisome number of institutions—may stave off bankruptcy in the short run, but it will seriously devalue higher education. It will give graduates little of lasting value in return for their costly investment and, thus, may in time further undermine public confidence and support.

Such a course only exacerbates higher learning's present crisis. It signals a retreat from the position of respect that has given colleges and universities a special place in the hierarchy of American institutions. This position depends less on wealth or political power than on a clarity of purpose and an integrity of mission that, save perhaps for the churches, is to be found in no other contemporary social institution.

Despite its present insecure position, we believe higher learning remains one of our best hopes for social progress and that its leadership is urgently required. But to fulfill its broader social mission, the academy must enlarge its vision and regain confidence in itself.

II

A TRADITION OF SERVICE

FOR OVER 300 YEARS in this country, higher learning and the larger purposes of society have been intertwined. It is an extraordinary testament to the early settlers' belief in education that our first college was established when the little colony on Massachusetts Bay was only six years old.

Harvard's purposes were clearly understood: train a literate ministry, educate future lawyers and civic leaders, and, more generally, perpetuate the tradition of humane learning in the New World. Without a deep commitment to serve God and man, Harvard could not have survived its lean and austere beginnings; an entire class typically consisted of fifteen to twenty students. Very early, public subsidy had to be provided for this institution that clearly served the public good. In 1652, the Massachusetts General Court donated land and later authorized special tax levies for Harvard's benefit.

As more colonial colleges were founded—William and Mary in 1693, Yale in 1701, and Princeton in 1751, to name only a few—these institutions began subtly but decisively to shape the nation's future. Their goals may not have been fully stated, but, in retrospect, they seem clear enough: to train not only the clergy but also a new educational leadership; to combat the restlessness of youth in a developing country; to instill in their students piety, loyalty, and responsible citizenship; and to transmit knowledge that would be useful, not merely in the classical sense of preparing gentlemen, but for the practical demands of a changing world.

Following the Revolution, the climate supported national expansion and minds were on the future. The patriot leader, Dr. Benjamin Rush, wrote: "The business of education has acquired a new complexion by the independence of the country. . . ." The nation's colleges, he predicted, would be "nurseries of wise and good men to adapt our modes of teaching to the peculiar form of government."[1]

The Eastern colleges were mostly in the hands of traditionalists, but the new frontier colleges had a flexibility unknown to the Old World. They were governed less by academic tradition than by the challenges of survival in the wilderness. Roused by the spirit of the frontier, and soon of America's "Manifest Destiny," old orthodoxies were challenged on the campus. The middling ranks of society—the merchants, tradesmen, skilled artisans, and ambitious farmers—were growing rapidly; and the newer colleges concluded that they could best serve the nation, and themselves, by helping these emerging groups.

Historian Frederick Rudolph has written of this generation of educators: "All were touched by the American faith in tomorrow, in the unquestionable capacity of Americans to achieve a better world."[2] He also wrote that Rensselaer Polytechnic Institute, one of the first technical schools in the country (founded in 1824), became "a constant reminder that the United States needed railroad builders, bridge builders, builders of all kinds, and that the Institute in Troy was prepared to create them even if the old institutions were not."[3]

The handwriting was on the wall. America's colleges would be of practical service to the nation. In 1846, the corporation at Yale authorized the creation of a professorship of "agricultural chemistry and animal and vegetable physiology."[4] In 1850, the reform-minded president of Brown University, Francis Wayland, urged his faculty, without success, to build a curriculum that would "benefit all classes."[5] At Harvard, in the same decade, President Edward Everett stressed the institution's role in the service of business and economic prosperity. Harvard took Everett's message to heart. A few years later, when historian Henry Adams asked his students why they had come to Cambridge, the answer he got was unambiguous: "The degree of Harvard College is worth money to me in Chicago."[6]

In the expansive climate of the nineteenth century, higher learning's position was remarkably enhanced by Congress' approval of the Morrill Act of 1862, later called the Land Grant College Act. This legislation provided federal land to each of the states to permit them, with the proceeds from its sale, to support not only education in the liberal arts, but also training in the skills that would undergird the nation's agricultural and mechanical revolutions.

The land-grant colleges were not the creation of academic genius or extraordinary governmental vision. Land speculators were probably more actively interested in seeing the Morrill Act passed than most educators. Congress itself gave approval to the bill in the heat of the Civil War, not so much to promote education as to devise a legislative package to unite the North and West against the rebels in the South.

Whatever the reasons for its passage, few laws relating to education have had a more far-reaching impact. These new colleges brought a practical approach to education that linked the classroom and the campus to national expansion. The existing network of private colleges on the Atlantic seaboard and small sectarian schools in the interior simply could not respond to America's convulsive social, economic, political, and technological changes. They could not answer the call of modern agriculture; they were not ready to train the engineers and technicians required by the industrial revolution.

And so, from Maine to California, a new kind of institution arose to fill the void. Lawrence Cremin wrote that the land-grant colleges "provided the beginning of a national network of educational research and development institutions that the federal government would subsequently use for a variety of enterprises, from the training of reserve officers for the armed forces, to the reform of agricultural production, to the renovation of rural community life."[7]

Something of the excitement of this era was captured in Willa Cather's description of her fellow students and teachers at the University of Nebraska in the 1890s:

> (They) came straight from the cornfields with only summer's wages in their pockets, hung on through four years, shabby and underfed, and completed the course by really heroic self-sacrifice. Our instructors were oddly assorted: wandering pioneer school teachers, stranded ministers of the Gospel, a few enthusiastic young men just out of graduate school. There was an atmosphere of endeavor, of expectancy and bright hopefulness about the young college that had lifted its head from the prairie only a few years ago.[8]

Not all agreed. Traditional educators looked with amused contempt, if not outright anger, at Ezra Cornell's pledge of the 1860s that he would found an institution "where any person can find instruction in any study."[9] They viewed as a betrayal of the academic mission the establishment of "agricultural experiment stations" to serve farmers. They ridiculed the "cow colleges," deplored the watering down of academic standards, and recoiled from the idea that large numbers of young people who were not of the established elite were going on to college. The conservative view was reflected in a sarcastic ditty:

> Education is the rage
>   in Wisconsin
> Everyone is wise and sage
>   in Wisconsin

Every newsboy that you see
Has a varsity degree
Every cook's a Ph.D.
　　in Wisconsin

Woodrow Wilson, professor of political economy at Princeton, was among the skeptics. In an 1896 essay somewhat ironically titled "Princeton in the Nation's Service," the future president insisted that higher learning was becoming far too practical in its focus. "Science," he warned, "has bred in us a spirit of experiment and contempt for the past.[10] It has made us credulous of quick improvement, hopeful of discovering panaceas, confident of success in every new thing." Wilson called upon the university to "illuminate duty by every lesson that can be drawn out of the past."[11]

But confidence "in every new thing" prevailed. Institutions once devoted primarily to teaching, and later to research, added *service* as a third important mission, which, in the nineteenth and early twentieth centuries, had a distinctly local flavor. After visiting Madison in 1909, Lincoln Steffens observed: "In Wisconsin, the university is as close to the intelligent farmer as his pig-pen or his tool-house; the university laboratories are part of the alert manufacturer's plant. . . ."[12]

During the twentieth century, American higher education grew more confident and strong as the nation, time and time again, turned to the campuses for help. Governor Robert La-Follette forged a link between the campus and the state that became known nationally as "The Wisconsin Idea." In the 1930s, when Franklin D. Roosevelt set out to rescue a faltering economy and, perhaps, democracy itself, he turned to the academy for help, popularizing the phenomenon known as the "brain trust." No president since has tried to lead the nation without tapping a pool of talent that only the campuses could provide.

When depression gave way to war, the universities joined with government to create a powerful scientific research engine such as the world had never before seen. At the beginning of World War II, delegations led by Vannevar Bush of M.I.T. and James Bryant Conant of Harvard volunteered to President Roosevelt the universities' help in bringing victory to the nation. The universities and the state had joined in common cause.

Bush, by then President of the Carnegie Institution of Washington, and chairman of the National Advisory Committee for Aeronautics, was eager to avoid the military supervision of civilian scientists. Consequently, he took the lead in establishing, in 1940, the National Defense Research Committee which, a year later, became the Office of Scientific Research and Development. Bush urged a continuing federal commitment to peacetime research; and, in his 1945 report to the president, he recalled successes of the recent past.

We all know how much the new drug, penicillin, has meant to our grievously wounded men on the grim battlefronts of this war—the countless lives it has saved—the incalculable suffering which its use has prevented. Science and the great practical genius of this Nation made this achievement possible.

Some of us know the vital role which radar has played in bringing the Allied Nations to victory over Nazi Germany and in driving the Japanese steadily back from their island bastions. Again it was painstaking scientific research over many years that made radar possible. What we often forget are the millions of pay envelopes on a peacetime Saturday night which are filled because new products and new industries have provided jobs for countless Americans. Science made that possible too.

Science, by itself, provides no panacea for individual, social, and economic ills. It can be effective in the national welfare only as a member of a team, whether the conditions be peace or war. But without scientific progress no amount of achievement in other directions can insure our health, prosperity, and security as a nation in the modern world.[13]

The case could not have been more clearly stated. Higher learning and government together had, through scientific collaboration, changed the course of history.

After the war, with some 12 million men returning to civilian life, the prospect of absorbing that mass of veterans into the domestic economy seemed bleak. The specter of large scale unemployment and still-fresh memories of the Great Depression sent Congress urgently searching for a solution, and campuses held a key. Through the G.I. Bill of Rights, which offered a college education to every veteran who wanted it, the nation's lawmakers simultaneously rewarded the young men (and some women) for service to their country, delayed their entry into the job market, and eventually returned them to civilian life with their minds enriched and their talents sharpened.

Many educators initially viewed with alarm this massive influx of older persons with life experiences of a most non-academic sort. Nevertheless, the challenge was accepted. Quonset huts, even tent cities, sprang up on campuses across the nation. The veterans enrolled with great enthusiasm and a clear sense of purpose. Far from being a disruptive force, as had been feared, they were an inspiration to their younger classmates. Even gray-haired academic traditionalists grew accustomed to campuses ringed by married-student housing full of baby carriages, playgrounds, and diaper service delivery vans.

For American higher education, a new chapter had begun. Practically overnight the G.I. Bill changed the entire tradition of who should attend college. Almost 8 million former World

War II servicemen and women benefitted from the legislation. In the years to come, younger brothers and sisters, neighborhood friends, nieces and nephews, and, eventually, sons and daughters, quite naturally expected to follow in the footsteps of the veterans.

The expansion of educational opportunity received another boost in the postwar years with the phenomenal growth of community colleges. These unique two-year institutions increased in the 1960s at the rate of about one every ten days. Offering tuition-free or low-cost education, they enabled many first-time college students to live at home or work part-time during their first two undergraduate years before transferring to a senior institution. In addition, community colleges trained a host of the nation's youth to enter a surprising array of occupations, ranging from medical assistant to electronics expert to engineering aide, or to take new positions in the burgeoning service industries. They also opened college doors to growing numbers of adults.

In the late 1950s and early 1960s, talent was mobilized in the unprecedented Marshall plan for European recovery. Significantly, that plan was first proposed by Secretary of State George C. Marshall in a commencement address at Harvard in 1947. Under its provisions, campus teams helped to reestablish civilian governments in the vanquished nations. Similar groups traveled overseas when, in 1949, President Truman made "Point Four" a cornerstone of American foreign policy. Not unlike the extension agents of the land-grant colleges, these experts worked with peasants in primitive villages, technicians in cities, and with civil servants in newly independent governments. They became America's peacetime emissaries to promote economic development in Third World countries.

A group of younger emissaries from the campuses followed. They were the pioneers to whom John F. Kennedy turned when he wanted to enlist American skills and idealism in this country's mission abroad. It was on the campus of the University of Michigan in 1960, that, as a young presidential candidate surrounded by students eager to help create a better world, he first proposed creation of the Peace Corps.

Shocked by the Soviet success in launching the first space satellite in 1957, Americans again turned to the schools and colleges to help fill a perceived gap in the instruction of science and mathematics. The nation's campuses responded once again to a new and vital public mission. The very title of the National Defense Education Act, proposed by President Eisenhower in 1958, clearly indicates the link between education and the security of the nation.

In the 1960s and 1970s, America's schools and colleges assumed a major role in the nation's unfinished business of ending racial discrimination and extending social justice. Recognizing the contributions of education to social and economic equality, the campuses rapidly expanded access to higher learning for women and members of racial minorities. In these two decades, the percentage of college students who were black increased from 6 to 10 and the percentage who were women increased from 39 to 51.[14] Gains in participation of women at advanced levels of higher education are particularly notable. Between 1968 and 1979, the percentage of graduate students who were women increased from 33 to 47, and the percentage of students in professional schools who are women increased from 6 to 27.[15] By 1967 half of all 18- and 19-year-old high school graduates were moving on to some form of higher education[16]—a remarkable record achieved by no other society. For millions of additional students, the colleges of the nation provided broadened opportunity.

In reviewing the achievements of higher education from the earliest days to the present we recognize that, for most of the past, the tasks for higher learning were vastly simpler, the student populations were more homogenous, and the expectations of the public more modest than they have been in recent years. It is also true that progress has not been without interruption. There have been times throughout our history when colleges were on the fringes of the national endeavor, struggling and ignored, or themselves insensitive to responsibilities for social progress. Moreover, even during periods of active involvement in national service, purposes and priorities were subjected to vigorous debate on campus.

Still, despite the inevitable conflicts and inherent tensions, there remains the inescapable conclusion that the nation has gained immensely from its strong and vital network of diverse campuses. Higher education has profited from the partnership as well. Campus confidence has grown precisely at those times when educators were called upon to participate in national crusades of consequence—to expand frontiers, to advance knowledge, to create a better and more just society, and to make the nation more secure.

B UT THERE IS ANOTHER, equally important strand woven into the American tradition of higher learning. Colleges and universities have also served the nation as centers of criticism, social protest, and dissent. In the antebellum period, Oberlin College played a key role in the abolitionist movement and was a well-known stop on the Underground Railroad. In the Progessive Era, hundreds of college students became residents of settlement houses in the immigrant slums, and supported other reform causes. College women were a mainstay of the suffrage movement on its way to ultimate victory in 1920. In the 1930s, college students marched and organized for peace.

The most dedicated recruits for the civil rights and antiwar movements of the 1950s and 1960s came from the nation's colleges. Students risked harsh legal penalties by staging lunch counter sit-ins in the South. In the "Freedom Summer" of 1962, thousands of idealistic northern students helped with black voter registration. Campus protesters led the attack against the Vietnam War that stirred a bitter backlash. The height of the national tension was reached in May 1970—with the tragedies of Kent State University in Ohio and Jackson State University in Mississippi in which six students were killed.

Over the years, America's campuses have sheltered advocates of unpopular social, political, and economic views. Whether it was Thorstein Veblen, C. Wright Mills, or Arthur Jensen, the American colleges and universities have respected the right of the minority opinion to be heard. While some faculty members have offered courses in business management, others on the same campus have published and taught radical critiques of capitalist society. Contradictory as that may seem, both activities have historically been a part of the academic tradition.

To be sure, the academy has not always acquitted itself well in respecting and protecting independent thinking. Even at some of the nation's most prestigious institutions, professors who opposed slavery, favored bimetalism, defended the theory of evolution, questioned American involvement in war, or held other dissenting opinions were dismissed, censured, or frightened into silence. During World War I, Columbia's President Nicholas Murray Butler dismissed some of the institution's most distinguished professors and silenced many others on the mere suspicion of their insufficiently enthusiastic support of the Allies' war aims. Sometimes the faculty itself has betrayed the principles of tolerance. At the University of Wisconsin during World War I, the faculty officially censured one of its greatest friends and supporters, Senator Robert M. LaFollette, for his opposition to America's role in the war.

At its best, however, higher learning has vigorously defended the right to dissent and to hold unpopular opinions. This issue led to the formation of the American Association of University Professors in 1915 and to its subsequent publication of a series of eloquent statements in defense of academic freedom. Harvard's president, James B. Conant, urged universities to shun secret research except in times of war, and thus to keep open the free exchange of scholarship. During the McCarthy era, with its demands for loyalty oaths and persecution of faculty members suspected of holding "un-American" views, vigorous defenders of campus integrity were hard to find. Still, a few of higher learning's most respected academic leaders could be heard. In California, Clark Kerr and David Saxon, for example, spoke out against loyalty oaths and undue political interference.

There is no reason to expect such tension ever to disappear. While responding to the national agenda, higher learning, at its best, also acts as conscience and critic of society, thus risking the displeasure of the established order. To some, the two strands of that tradition—the academy as both servant and critic of society—may seem violently contradictory. We, however, are convinced that both strands are equally essential. Taken together they form a remarkable record of service to the nation.

The story of America and the story of higher learning are interwoven, and because of this intimate relationship, both the academy and the nation have been enriched. But how is the role of higher education to be redefined in terms that do not merely recall the past, but anticipate and respond adequately to the nation's future? This is the urgent question colleges and universities must now confront.

Section Two

IN THE NATION'S FUTURE

III

EDUCATING A NEW GENERATION

STUDENTS are at the heart of the academic enterprise and higher learning must commit itself, with urgency and dedication, to serve effectively a new generation of young Americans. To achieve this goal, standards of excellence at every level of schooling must be established and maintained.

Historically, Americans have had an almost touching faith in the value of education for their children. Over 130 years before the Declaration of Independence, the Massachusetts Bay Colony passed a law requiring every town or village of 50 or more souls to provide, at public expense, a schoolmaster to teach all the children to read and write. And it was characteristic of the New World that each generation was expected to do better than its parents—not simply to follow in their footsteps as was the norm in the Old World, but to outdistance them by striking out, breaking new paths, and striving for new goals.

This belief in education was, at times, unrealistic. Social class has never been absent in American society, and education alone has not always been the ladder to success. Still, as the human base of education broadened, so did the nation's reservoir of talent. While other Western industrial countries continued to sort out, at an early age, and eliminate from further study great numbers of their young people, the United States kept options open. As a result, an even greater proportion of youths from poor and working class homes completed high school, entered college, and moved on to careers that had not been open to their elders. The now familiar story of the laborer or sharecropper, the waiter or cab driver whose son—and increasingly, whose daughter—became a doctor, lawyer, scientist, or corporate or political leader is as basic to the strength of this society as any economic game plan.

Recently, however, the mood has changed. Today we hear a rising chorus of complaints about the quality of schooling. We see a national rush to reduce investment in education—with teacher layoffs, reductions in federal school assistance, and cutbacks in student aid. This flagging commitment reflects frustration over falling test scores, conflicts over national priorities, taxpayer revolts, and recognition that education is not a panacea to cure every social ill. Now is the time, some argue, to limit support for education and build up the *nonhuman* capital of the nation.

We conclude, however, that in the decade of the 1980s, it would be a grave mistake for this nation to shift resources disproportionately away from education and to forsake the public schools where 90 percent of our children are now enrolled. Today, as in the past, a new generation of young Americans must be intellectually well-trained.

Because of declining birth rates, the number of 18–24 year olds in the United States will drop 23 percent by 1997.[1] This means that fewer young people will be available to do the nation's work. The potential of every young adult must be fully developed, and more, not less, education will be urgently required.

Further, the ethnic and racial composition of young America is changing. While the population *as a whole* is aging, the youth population among black and Hispanic Americans remains large and will proportionately increase. Today, slightly more than one-quarter of white Americans are under 18 years of age, but nearly one-half of all Hispanics and over one-third of all blacks fall into this youth category (Graph A).

These demographic trends have special significance for the

24

GRAPH A

Distribution of Youth Under 18 by Ethnic Group
1980

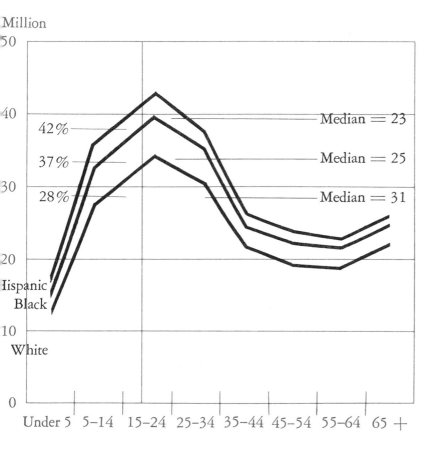

Million

50

40

42%   Median = 23

37%   Median = 25

30

28%   Median = 31

20

Hispanic
Black

10

White

0
Under 5   5–14   15–24   25–34   35–44   45–54   55–64   65 +

Source: Compiled by The Carnegie Foundation for the Advancement of Teaching using projections developed by the U.S. Bureau of Census and the Population Reference Bureau.

25

GRAPH B

Proportion of U.S. Households with
School-Age Children by Ethnic Group
1979

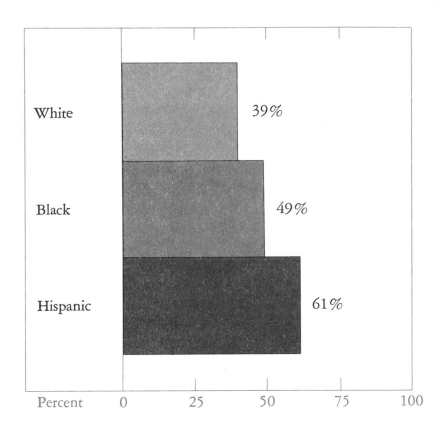

White 39%

Black 49%

Hispanic 61%

Percent 0   25   50   75   100

Source: U.S. Bureau of the Census. *Household and Family Charac-
teristics: March 1979.* Current Population Reports, Series P-20,
no. 352, 1980.

nation's colleges and schools. Since 1970, the proportion of black high school students in New York City has risen from 30 to 40 percent; Hispanic enrollments increased from 21 to 26 percent of the total. In the same period, the percentage of students in Milwaukee high schools who were white dropped from 75 to 34. Changes in the ethnic composition of high schools have been especially dramatic in Miami. In 1970, whites comprised 61 percent of the high school enrollment in that Florida city; today they comprise 36 percent. In 1978, of the twenty largest urban school districts in the United States, 12 had more than 50 percent minority enrollments.[2]

As the black and Hispanic share of the youth cohort is enlarged, education is affected in another way as well. In 1979, only 39 percent of all white households had school-age children. In contrast, nearly half (49 percent) of all black and 61 percent of all Hispanic households had school-age children (Graph B). With fewer school-age children, white America's commitment to education may well decline. At the same time, minority parents with more young children have a growing stake in education, yet historically they have had limited political and economic power.

Of special concern is the fact that black and Hispanic young people are precisely those with whom most of our nation's colleges and schools have been least successful. In 1979, 80 percent of white nineteen-year olds in the U.S. were high school graduates. However, that same year, 64 percent of black and 60 percent of Hispanic nineteen-year olds held high school diplomas.[3]

If minority students continue to leave school at the current rate, 150,000 additional young people—the equivalent of eleven entering freshman classes at giant Ohio State University—will lose their opportunity for further education by 1990. An increasing proportion of our youth will be condemned to social and economic failure. To avoid such tragic human waste, the rising generation of Americans must be adequately prepared for the world they will inherit.

For most of this century, the American system worked reasonably well for those students who attended. A high school education was considered adequate for all but a small number of professional pursuits. Recently, however, all this has changed. The base of the economy is shifting. Many old jobs have all but disappeared and new ones have emerged. If this society desires higher intellectual and economic productivity, a larger stock of both nonhuman *and* human capital will be needed.

Indeed, as we look ahead, it seems likely that even 12 years of formal schooling—as a terminal program—will be inadequate for most students. Fifteen years ago, Gunnar Myrdal predicted that by the year 2000: "practically all American youths would . . . demand and obtain not only secondary but also college education of some kind."[4] Myrdal's prediction seems closer to realization today.

It is our conclusion that, from now on, almost all young people will, at some time in their lives, need some form of post-secondary school education if they are to remain economically productive and socially functional in a world whose tasks and tools are becoming increasingly complex.

Between 1950 and 1979, the proportion of professional and technical workers in the workforce increased from 9 to 16 percent, and the proportion of managers and administrators grew from 9 to 11 percent. At the same time, the percentage of blue collar workers decreased from 37 to 33, while farm workers, as a proportion of the labor force, plummeted from 12 to 3 percent. Only in one category—service workers—was there an increase in the jobs in the workforce for which post-high school education might not initially be required.[5]

This trend toward more specialized work seems to be accelerating. Employment in the five principal occupations associated with the computer field grew from 765,000 in 1970 to

1,158,000 in 1978—two and one-half times the overall growth rate in the nation's work force.[6]

There will, of course, continue to be a number of dreary, dead-end jobs, and technology will continue to make some work intellectually less demanding. The new technology may, in fact, be creating a two-tiered work force with job training requirements increasing for some workers while decreasing for others. The computational skills once required of the bank teller or the department store clerk, for example, are rapidly being supplanted by scanners and computers.

But when all of this has been acknowledged, the fact remains that more education and perhaps a different kind of education, will be needed if a new generation of Americans is to become productively employed and find satisfaction in a world dominated by new, more complicated tools.

One can think of specific sectors, such as the military, where equipment has already become more sophisticated than the available labor force and where buying more hardware seems unwise unless accompanied by at least a comparable investment in the people who will have to use it. In the Navy, 75 percent of the billets in 1977 require skilled or highly skilled personnel. In 1980, the Navy required almost twice as large a percentage of highly skilled personnel as it did in 1945 (42 percent vs. 23 percent).[7]

The need for better educated and technically well-trained military personnel is strikingly illustrated in the almost incredible increase in the number of pages in technical manuals used for the upkeep of the various naval aircraft. The manual for the F-6F of World War II had 950 pages; the F-14 of 1975 requires thousands of pages of technical information.[8]

This is not to say that institutions of higher learning should only prepare technicians, or that the nation's colleges and schools should be viewed as a feeder system for the Department of Defense. Rather, we are underscoring the fact that the workplace is changing dramatically, that traditional notions about prework preparation are becoming obsolete, and that more education will be required to meet the nation's diverse social and economic needs.

The tendency to ignore these realities is deeply alarming. We find it sadly ironic that at a time when productivity is being so heavily stressed by our political leaders, the term so often seems to mean simply the output of our factories, mines, forests, and oil wells, as if such output can, somehow, be divorced from people. The failure adequately to educate—at public expense—a new generation of students, would be a shocking denial of their rights and a fatal undermining of the vital interests of the nation.

The conclusion is clear. Higher learning must redouble its efforts to meet more effectively the needs of those who have been inadequately served by education in the past.

As a first step, we urge close collaboration between the nation's colleges and schools. A century ago educators understood better than we do today that you cannot have excellence in higher education without excellence in the schools. In 1884, the Massachusetts Classical and High School Teachers' Association unanimously passed a resolution that deplored the lack of cooperation between high schools and colleges. They invited nineteen New England college presidents to meet with them, and at this first high school/college conclave a national panel called "The Committee of Ten" was established. In 1894, President Eliot of Harvard commented that "The Committee's greatest promise of usefulness" lay in its "obvious tendency to promote cooperation among school and college teachers" to advance "comprehensive education reforms."[9]

In 1908, Abraham Flexner of The Carnegie Foundation for the Advancement of Teaching described the schools as the source of "the raw material" with which "colleges must work."[10] In 1945, the celebrated Harvard Red Book suggested that it is impossible to talk about general education at the college level without also looking at curriculum in the schools.[11] Shocked by the Soviet launching of Sputnik, gifted high school and college teachers came together in the 1950s to work out sequential courses of study in mathematics, English, biology, and physics.

Schooling in America is in serious trouble; and higher education has a responsibility to help solve the crisis it has, through neglect and inadvertence, helped create. We cannot have quality in our colleges if during the twelve preceding years of formal education the teaching is inadequate and the curriculum lacks coherence.

Schools and colleges should once again give top priority to the effective use of language; and all students, during the first, crucial years of formal education, must learn to read and write and compute with skill. These are the fundamentals for all future learning. A rigorous and balanced core curriculum must be developed through which students at both the school and the college levels learn about their heritage, the natural world, and the social and technological environment in which they live. Students in the upper years of high school should be given the opportunity to test their aptitudes and devote a portion of their program to a special interest field. Above all, colleges must recognize the centrality of teaching. The quality of teachers recruited for the nation's classrooms must improve. Teacher training programs must be dramatically overhauled, and the rewards of teaching—not only salaries but social recognition—must be greatly enhanced.

There are no panaceas, to be sure. Still, rebuilding quality in education is an urgent matter, since the real problem confronts not schools, but students whose lives will be shaped by the programs we provide. "In every child who is born . . . ," James Agee once wrote, "the potentiality of the human race is born again."[12] Educating a new generation of Americans to

31

their full potential is higher learning's most compelling obligation.

IV

GENERATING NEW KNOWLEDGE

I N ITS SERVICE to the nation, higher education faces yet another challenge: to defend and strengthen scholarly investigation, the soil of creative thought in which the entire learning enterprise is rooted. America's colleges and universities must convince the public, and perhaps some of their own constituencies, of the urgent need to generate new knowledge and search for solutions to vexing problems.

The mission of scholarly research came late to higher education. When President Jefferson sought a scientific leader for the first of the great Western explorations, he did not go to the colleges, where science was not yet well-developed. Instead, he looked within government and selected his personal secretary, Meriwether Lewis.[1] In the early years of the Republic, most scientific work was done by gifted amateurs without academic affiliation: people like Jefferson himself; the brilliant mathematician, Nathaniel Bowditch; the pioneer botanists, John and William Bartram; or the intrepid astronomer, Maria Mitchell, who set up an observatory on lonely Nantucket and, one October night in 1847, discovered a new comet.

The land-grant colleges, from their earliest days, related scholarly endeavor to the practical demands of the frontier. By the mid-19th century, the independent Atlantic seaboard colleges were slowly beginning to transform themselves into research institutions. At Harvard, the Lawrence Scientific School and, at Yale, the Sheffield Scientific School, were forerunners of a historic commitment to research in the natural sciences. The

Massachusetts Institute of Technology opened its doors at the end of the Civil War, and soon was recognized as a research center. Johns Hopkins University, started in 1876, consciously modeled its entire program on the great European universities with their emphasis on graduate education and research.

The names of the thousands of distinguished university researchers who have added lustre to the nation's intellectual life would surely include heroic figures of earlier days—men like Yale chemist, Benjamin Silliman; the Harvard naturalist, Louis Agassiz; and astronomer, William Cranch Bond; the Amherst geologist, Edward Hitchcock; and the Columbia anthropologist, Franz Boas. It would also include giants of today, including such diverse scholars as M.I.T.'s Norbert Weiner, a pioneer in development of the computer; economist Paul Samuelsen at the same institution; Harvard's James Watson, who helped unlock the genetic code; Cal Tech's great chemist, Linus Pauling; M.I.T.'s Noam Chomsky, who transformed the field of linguistics; and the whole host of nuclear physicists and chemists—Lawrence, Urey, McMillan, Seaborg, and the others—who, on campuses across the land, did the basic research that reshaped our thinking and changed our world.

Since 1945, Americans have won more than half the Nobel Prizes awarded for science; they dominate the world's scientific and technical literature, producing, it is estimated, about 40 percent of the influential scholarly articles each year;[2] citations of American articles are about 30 percent higher than average.[3] Whereas American scientists once had to complete their training in other countries, now the reverse is true: between 1960 and 1974 foreign students received 19 percent of the science and engineering doctorates awarded by American universities.[4]

In reciting progress from research, we can now add that smallpox and polio have been eradicated and that the average yields of wheat and corn doubled between 1950 and 1975.[5] Recent developments of microconductors promise to revolutionize communications, and advances in psychopharmacy vastly improve treatment of schizophrenia and depression.

In our lifetime, we have witnessed the birth of the atomic age, with all its promise and hazards. We have sent men into outer space and watched them walk on the moon through the wonder of television, which also was unknown 50 years ago. We flew from New York to San Francisco in 12, then 8, then 5 hours. Travelers now leave Paris in the morning and reach New York in time for lunch. Electronic brains that filled whole rooms 30 years ago can now be carried in our pockets. As Henry Adams gloomily recognized 80 years ago, the changes brought about by research and subsequent innovations are almost overwhelming.

In his Harvard Phi Beta Kappa essay on the Uncertainty of Science, Lewis Thomas wrote:

> The great body of science, built, like a vast hill over the past three hundred years, is a mobile, unsteady structure, made up of solid-enough single bits of information, but with all the bits already moving about, fitting together in different ways, adding new bits to themselves with flourishes of adornment as though consulting a mirror.
>
> This is how we fell into the way of science. The endeavor is not, as is sometimes thought, a way of building a solid, indestructible body of immutable truth, fact laid precisely upon fact in the manner of twigs in an anthill. Science is not like this at all: it keeps changing, shifting, revising, discovering what is wrong and then heaving itself explosively apart to redesign everything. It is a living thing, a celebration of human fallibility. At its very best, it is rather like an embryo.[6]

The restless, probing mind of the researcher, so eloquently

evoked by Lewis, is an enormously important asset to the nation. The process of scholarly investigation never ends. Each new discovery poses new problems, opens up new options, and reminds us in a fascinating and frustrating way, that, with all of our supposed wisdom, we are only learning how to learn.

The issues that still perplex—now global in scale—are, if anything, more awesome than in the past, and there is no turning back. In 1980, The Council on Environmental Quality and the State Department issued *The Global 2000 Report.* Three years in the making, the report depicted a world "more crowded, more polluted, less stable ecologically, and more vulnerable to disruption than the world we live in."[7] *The Global 2000 Report* has been praised and criticized, but one central, unspoken message remains unchallenged: Man's quest for knowledge cannot be relaxed. We must know more about our own human resources, the physical universe, about our social and political systems, about our own human resources, about how the earth's resources can most efficiently be used, and how our heritage can be more fully understood.

There are ominous signs that, with of all the urgent national and international challenges we confront, our commitment to basic research is flagging. Between 1965 and 1977, as a proportion of the Gross National Product, total national expenditures for research and development declined by 24 percent, rising only by about 1 percent between 1978 and 1980;[8] from 1964 to 1980, federal expenditures for research and development declined by a startling 43 percent.[9] The American Association for the Advancement of Science reports that the proposed 12.5 percent increase in federal support to universities and colleges for research would still leave them well behind the expected rate of inflation for the period.[10]

The tendency to undervalue scholarship in the social sciences and humanities is especially distressing. Scholarly research in these fields is vital to the nation; yet in 1980, support for social science research amounted to only 4 percent of all federal research funds awarded to higher education. That same year, the National Science Foundation allocated only $31.4 million (3.2 percent of its total research funds) for social science research. In 1981, the amount dropped to $23.6 million, 2.3 percent of NSF's research funds. Currently, the Administration is asking Congress to appropriate $10 million for social science research in 1982. This would give social science less than 1 percent of NSF's total research budget of $1.033 billion.[11]

While federal research support to universities declines, industry-based research shows steady growth. During 1979, United States business and industry spent nearly $38 billion on research and development—a 13 percent increase over the previous year. This was about 70 percent of the total U.S. research and development outlay that year.[12] At its research and development center in Niskayuna, New York, General Electric employs 2,000 people, nearly 800 of them scientists and engineers.[13] Last year at Niskayuna and at 100 other G.E. laboratories, the corporation spent $1.6 billion for research and development.[14] That figure, for only one company, is more than 60 percent greater than the $975,130,000 spent by the National Science Foundation for its entire program in 1980.

Until now, university research supported by business and industry has been modest. In 1978, for example, industry gave only an estimated $85 million to universities for research. This figure was less than 3 percent of higher education's total research expenditures that year, and it represented an actual decrease from 1960, when corporate support stood at 5.5 percent.

However, it is likely that universities will increasingly turn to the private sector as federal research support declines. There are, we believe, grave risks in that prospect. The corporate world, by its very nature, seeks higher profits. Hence, "basic" research, in which universities excel, will be most attractive to corporations if its potential uses seem to be profitable at

37

the outset. This prior commitment to the utility of research conflicts, of course, with what basic research is all about.

Industrial secrecy and competition within business could have a chilling effect on access to new knowledge. In the past, issues of secrecy have been confined largely to classified defense-related research. Most universities have dealt with the problem by rejecting such contracts except in wartime. The secrecy issue in any industry-university alliance may be equally troublesome. Protecting commercial or industrial discoveries may be necessary in a competitive market place, thus undermining the open exchange of research findings so fundamental in an academic setting. We conclude that any commercially imposed restriction on research would not only violate the principle of academic freedom but could also inhibit and dampen the university's atmosphere of openness.

Traditionally, academic researchers have relied on a built-in system of peer criticism and evaluation. Networks of academics review the investigative process, scrutinize new work, and share ideas informally and at professional meetings. The goal is continuous quality control; but that system does not work if information is withheld from publication.

A still greater danger is that research initiative could shift from the individual scholar to the corporate manager—and that the professional future of the scientist might be linked more to an ability to please the patron than to his or her ability to ask important questions. In his historic plea for a federal commitment to basic research in peacetime, Vannevar Bush wrote:

> The scientist doing basic research may not be at all interested in the practical applications of his work, yet the further progress of industrial development would eventually stagnate if basic scientific research were long neglected.

38

The publicly and privately supported colleges, universities and research institutes are the centers of basic research. They are the wellspring of knowledge and understanding. As long as they are vigorous and healthy and their scientists are free to pursue the truth wherever it may lead, there will be a flow of new scientific knowledge to those who can apply it to practical problems of government, or in industry, or elsewhere.[15]

The involvement of commercial organizations in university-industry research is potentially compromising; yet we expect it to increase. Despite the risks we have described, corporate support frequently comes with few burdensome administrative controls and detailed regulations. There is clear benefit for universities and corporations to share costly equipment and supplies. Donald Kennedy, president of Stanford University, told a Congressional Committee that "commercial interest in basic research, whether it involves the attraction of scientists to industry or increased support of academic work by industry, will add a new and needed source of funding for such work at a time at which it is especially needed."[16]

As the research agenda crosses interdisciplinary lines, new networks of knowledge that link commercial and noncommercial laboratories inevitably may emerge. Indeed, in the future, the entire complex system of scholarly communication may undergo a major change. Could, for example, the potential of new technology for almost instantaneous exchange of ideas from one laboratory or scientist to another stimulate scholars to ask new questions that were not even evident before?

Kennedy, in concluding his Congressional testimony, said that basic research in universities "needs more, not less, relationship to industry. But I believe the conditions for that relationship need to be carefully structured, if the highly efficient mechanism for doing basic research is not to be unwittingly damaged." [17] We agree. Corporate funding or any other special interest funding, must not be allowed to dominate university research. In the university, with its relative openness, researchers are free to inquire, investigate, and challenge in ways that more closely approximate truth-seeking than any other process available to us.

Universities and colleges don't just produce knowledge—which many places do—but on the campus, research becomes synonymous with a quest for truth. That is a precious quality at a time when knowledge itself is increasingly politicized to support preconceived positions and special interests. Therefore, we conclude that the most suitable links between academic research and American industry would involve only research that can be pursued under the full control of the investigator whose success is judged by academic peers.

Those who seriously entertain the idea of allowing higher education's research function to diminish or shift to other sectors need to be reminded that the campus is where future scholars are prepared. Scholarly inquiry, Professor Wayne Booth has argued, is a tradition that cannot be interrupted without serious, perhaps irreparable damage. It is conceivable that in 1990, there will be no young professoriate; a link in the chain will be missing. Without adequate support, we face the grim prospect of losing a generation of scholars that can never be replaced.

Thus, much is at stake when higher learning's dominant position in research is threatened. Scholars in increasing numbers may be enticed to leave their university positions in favor of higher salaries and the promise of a more continuous flow of funds in industry. If accelerated, this trend would not only undermine the university's strength in research itself; it would draw the most valuable teaching talent away from campuses, thus completing a vicious circle.

In the final analysis, research is a creative response to anything we fail to understand and yearn to know. Much of the university's future engagement with the riddles of the world will involve the flash of insight that comes only after the intellect has been disciplined in the tradition that the educator has a responsibility to pass on. Research in its purest forms is to be found in American universities, where it cannot be allowed to languish or starve. Sustaining that creative process is absolutely crucial if higher learning is to be truly "in the nation's service."

V

ADVANCING CIVIC LEARNING

THIS NATION began with a conviction, at once deceptively simple and profound, that, for democracy to work, education is essential. When Thomas Jefferson was asked if mass opinion could be trusted, he responded, "I know of no safe depository of the ultimate powers of society but the people themselves. And if we think them not enlightened enough to exercise their control with a wholesome discretion, the remedy is not to take it from them, but to inform their discretion."[1] We believe that the advancement of civic learning must become one of higher education's most essential goals.

The Jeffersonian vision of a democracy sustained by enlightened citizens seemed within our grasp when values were more widely shared, when society was more cohesive, and when public policy issues were more simple to grasp. But the vision of a grassroots democracy that so captured the imagination of Alexis de Tocqueville when he visited America in the 1830s seems today increasingly Utopian. As early as 1922, in a book called *Public Opinion,* Walter Lippmann warned that public ignorance of increasingly complex problems was democracy's greatest challenge, and in the last 60 years, the problem has grown more acute. Issues facing the electorate have become enormously complex and government seems increasingly remote. Today, many Americans are shockingly ill-informed about public issues—when they are aware of them at all.

Closely linked to this issue, we believe, is the declining confidence in our public institutions. Between 1964 and 1972, citizen alienation in this country substantially increased, and the disturbing pattern persists even as the Vietnam and Watergate traumas fade. In the latest presidential election, only 52 percent of the nation's eligible voters—the lowest turnout since 1948—went to the polls. If public opinion surveys are to be believed, half of the Americans (51 percent) today do *not* believe that important national problems such as energy shortages, inflation, and crime can be solved through traditional American political institutions and 50 percent do *not* believe that the electoral process is the principal determinant of how the country is actually run.[2]

The proportion of citizens professing "great confidence" in the leaders of major social institutions fell from 45 percent in 1966 to 21 percent in 1979. Confidence in the executive branch of government fell from 41 to 17 percent; in the Congress from 42 to 18 percent. But the sharpest drops in confidence were in several of our most hallowed leaders and institutions. The number of people willing to express trust in physicians went from 73 percent in 1966 to 30 percent in 1979. Confidence in higher education leaders dropped nearly in half— from 61 percent to 33 percent.[3]

Disaffection also permeates the campus. In his provocative book, *When Dreams and Heroes Died,* Arthur Levine reports that most entering freshmen "believe that all social institutions, from large corporations to the church, are at least somewhat immoral or dishonest." Adds Levine: "Campus interviews at twenty-six colleges across the nation show that this feeling is strongest among the young, who have never experienced better times." [4]

A recent survey also reveals that a significant percentage of college freshmen, like the rest of the populace, distrusts many of the nation's basic social institutions (Table 1).

TABLE 1. Percentage of college freshmen who think national institutions are considerably dishonest or immoral.

Major corporations	41
Major labor unions	41
Congress	39
President and administration	37
National news media	36
Police and law-enforcement agencies	31
Courts and justice system	24
Public schools	23
U.S. military	21
Colleges and universities	20
Churches	18

Source: Bachman and Johnston, 1979, p. 86. Reprinted from *Psychology Today* magazine. Copyright Ziff-Davis Publishing Company.

Another campus observer, Professor Clarence Mondale of George Washington University, assessing college student attitudes, finds a startling shift since the early 1970s from involvement to indifference.

> "Ten years ago," he notes, "students were actively engaged, caught up, almost in spite of themselves, in the general student unrest. Now they have withdrawn from all that. . . . They are good at asserting their limited interests. They are especially clear about their limits. Most of the old issues of conscience are still there:

race, women's rights, population, environment. Most sentiments about such issues among these students is 'right'—they hope things will work out well. The drift is toward political indifference." [5]

We do not believe that this lack of confidence in our institutions is fully justified. The United States may be problem-ridden but it's strength, vitality, and resources of the spirit remain formidable. We suggest that the detachment and mistrust derive, at least in part, from the pace of social change and a great gap between public issues and public understanding.

As citizens, we find ourselves almost overwhelmed. The information needed to think constructively about the agenda of government seems increasingly beyond our grasp. Should our use of nuclear energy be expanded or cut back? Can an adequate supply of water be assured? How can the spiralling arms race be brought under control? What is a "safe" level of atmospheric pollution? Even the semi-metaphysical question of when a human life begins has become an item on the political agenda.

In 1979, millions of Americans sat uneasily in front of their television sets as the Three Mile Island crisis unfolded, listening to strange talk about "rems" and "cold shutdowns," in what sounded like a foreign language. The truth is, it *was* a foreign language. Most viewers had no reference points to give meaning to terms that were suddenly of grave concern. More recently, citizens have tried with similar bafflement to follow the debate over the MX missile, with its highly technical jargon of deterrence and counter-deterrence. Even what once seemed to be reasonable local matters—zoning regulations, school desegregation, drainage problems, public transportation issues, licensing requests from competing cable TV companies —call for specialists who debate technicalities and frequently confuse rather than clarify the issues.

Today, public policy circuits appear to be dangerously

overloaded. In frustration, many Americans now seek simple solutions to complex problems, they turn to repressive censorship, align themselves with narrowly focused special-interest groups, retreat into nostalgia for a world that never was, succumb to the blandishments of glib electronic soothsayers, or—worst of all—simply withdraw completely, convinced that nothing can be done. It is no longer possible, many argue, to resolve complex public issues through the democratic process. How, they ask, can citizens debate policy choices of consequence when they do not even know the language?

As a nation, we are becoming civically illiterate. Unless we find better ways to educate ourselves *as citizens,* we run the risk of drifting unwittingly into a new kind of Dark Age—a time when small cadres of specialists will control knowledge and thus control the decision-making process. These high priests of technology will understand, or claim to understand, the complicated issues, telling us what we should believe and how we should act. In this new age of growing confusion, citizens would make critical decisions, not on the basis of what they know, but on the basis of blind faith in one or another set of professed experts.

For those who care about government "by the people," this upsurge of apathy and decline in public understanding cannot go unchallenged. In a world where human survival is at stake, ignorance is not an acceptable alternative. The replacement of democratic government by a technocracy or the control of policy by special-interest groups is not tolerable.

We are convinced that both formal and informal education must rise to meet the challenge. Specifically, we believe that tired old academic workhorse "civics" must be updated and restored in the curriculum to what was once an honored place.

Obviously, no one institution in society can single-handedly deal with this massive challenge. Beyond the classroom, churches, libraries, youth groups, labor unions, senior citizens' organizations, and many other groups should become greater sources of civic education. The media—newspapers, journals, radio, and television—also have a powerful role to play.

But it is equally clear that the nation's schools, colleges, and universities have a special obligation to combat growing illiteracy about public issues. Without any dilution of academic rigor, we believe civic understanding can be increased through courses ranging from literature and art to nuclear physics and industrial engineering. A better grounding in rhetoric and logic, and in the techniques of discussion and debate would also help prepare responsible citizens. Students should critically encounter the classic political thinkers from Plato, Hobbes, Locke, and Montesquieu to John Adams, James Madison, and John C. Calhoun. But, equally important, they should study government today, not just by examining its theory and machinery, but by exploring current public issues.

Our purpose here is not to propose a special curricular agenda, but to call attention to an urgent problem. Schools and colleges simply must help students understand the process by which public policy is shaped and prepare them to make informed, discriminating judgments on questions that will affect the nation's future.

CIVIC EDUCATION is not just a one-shot affair. If Americans are to be more adequately informed, *education for citizenship must become a lifelong process.* As Eric Ashby has observed, the difference between educating for citizenship in the nineteenth century and today is that the nineteenth century graduate "could assume that he would grow old in a world familiar to him as a youth." Continues Ashby: "We are living in the first era for which this assumption is false, and we have not yet faced the consequences of this fact."[6] Humanity has, of course, always lived with change, even in the 19th Century, but the rate of change today is very great. A major challenge for higher education is to find ways to combat built-in obsolescence.

Traditionally, schooling has been viewed as a prework ritual. The goal was to provide, during one continuous pre-adult experience, the information and skills needed to live a satisfying and productive life. At commencement time—whether high school or college—formal learning was completed. Most students left campus never to return, except perhaps for an occasional sentimental reunion. Today, this pattern has begun to shift. Life expectancy has increased from 47 years in 1900 to 74 years in 1980. By the year 2000, it is estimated that nearly 30 percent of Americans will be over the age of 50.

Older people now retire earlier, live longer, and for many, scholarship is becoming a lifelong pursuit. In the five years between 1973 and 1979, the number of college students in the 35-and-over age group increased from 787,000 to 1.4 million.[7] As more and more adults return to campus—for degrees, for training in new careers, or for cultural enrichment—continuing education has become a booming business.

But this picture has a darker side. While older students are going back to school, the sad fact is that, on many campuses, lifelong learning remains a program without purpose. Adult education courses grow like Topsy—but goals are not well-defined. Mail order degrees, and a smorgasbord of electives are offered with little concern for quality or coherence. A major university's continuing education catalog that arrived in the mail recently contained a list of some 55 courses offered during the current term ranging from "The Dermatologist Discusses Skin Care" and "Stock Market and Tax Shelters" to "The Art of Meditation" and "Assertiveness Training." Only three courses were even remotely connected to the civic responsibilities of adults, and even this is stretching things a bit. One of them was titled "Your Income Tax and New Legislation."

Older students, just like undergraduates, have a variety of interests and they should be offered many options. K. Patricia Cross found in her landmark study of adult learners that vocational and "hobby" courses are consistently the most popular with adults.[8] But this simply may reflect, at least in part, a failure of institutional wisdom. If adult education were taken more seriously by colleges, it would be taken more seriously by students. When adults are asked to list topics in which they have an *interest,* general education and public affairs rank high.[9] We find it noteworthy that when CBS Television presented a five-part, prime-time special on the military and national security not long ago, millions of Americans watched the program and it stirred widespread debate. Clearly, adults care deeply about consequential public issues.

In the 1980s and beyond, the majority of the students being served by higher education will be over 21 years of age. Adult education programs must be developed with clearly stated goals, something more than pastime diversions or warmed-over undergraduate offerings. In a world where the decisions confronting citizens have awesome implications, educating adults and helping to create a sense of commonweal becomes an urgent obligation. Specifically, *we propose that the nation's colleges and universities become systematically engaged in the civic education of adults.*

We do not propose that adult education be reduced to endless seminars on world affairs. However, civic education seems to us to have a special place in this emerging program. What we need, perhaps, is a new adult education degree—a bachelor's or master's in civic education—to give this new priority the stature and credibility it deserves.

Such an adult degree program would require careful planning and support by faculty. The aim would be to increase understanding of policy formation and more responsible citizen participation. We can envision an interdisciplinary approach—

one with courses from a variety of departments—political science, literature, the history of science, comparative government, ethics, philosophy, and the like. Each semester all students in the program might also come together in a common seminar on public policy. One such seminar might focus on classic texts of political thought. Another might examine a contemporary civic issue from an international perspective. The "laboratory" or "case-study" model also might be followed, with students using original documents and other source materials to probe one specific issue in depth.

Such a "case-study" seminar might focus first on an historical event—the decision of President Andrew Jackson to remove the Native American population from Georgia and other southern states, for example. How was this decision made? What political, constitutional, social, and cultural forces shaped it? What alternatives were available? Seminar members might then turn to a contemporary issue: defense policy, tax reform, Social Security, health care, nuclear power, or a subject of community concern: low-income housing, electoral redistricting, a plan to build a new hospital, or a proposal to construct a condominium on a choice lakefront site.

Both specialists and politicians might be invited to debate the issues. The faculty committee responsible for the new degree program might also develop a contemporary issues lecture series, open to both campus and community.

This program, we believe, would be appropriate for all citizens. In addition, colleges and universities have a special obligation to continue to educate society's policy makers: journalists, corporate directors, congressional and legislative staff members, judges, senior civil servants, labor leaders, and clergymen, for example. Public policy programs for these specialists, like those for other people, can be offered in a variety of ways—through weekend seminars, special institutes, and "alumni colleges" that bring graduates back to campus for short-term courses.

While civic education is always important, it will become increasingly significant during an era of constraint. In times of affluence and expansion, new, bold Great Society projects could be launched while hard choices were ignored. Today we are discovering that painful choices *must* be made: between health and defense budgets, between tax cuts and welfare programs, between more energy consumption and clean air. And we are beginning to understand that the consequences of today's actions will be long lasting and profound. As the stakes increase, civic education becomes urgent and even more consequential than before.

In 1896, Woodrow Wilson, then a forty-year-old professor of jurisprudence and political economy, wrote in the previously cited essay:

> ". . . the spirit of service will give college a place in the public annals of the nation. It is indispensable, it seems to me, if it is to do its right service, that the air of affairs should be admitted to all its classrooms. I do not mean the air of party politics, but the air of the world's transactions . . . . There is laid upon us the compulsion of the national life. We dare not keep aloof and closet ourselves while a nation comes to its maturity. The days of glad expansion are gone, our life grows tense and difficult; our resource for the future lies in careful thought, providence, and a wise economy; and the school must be of the nation."[10]

These words, it seems to us, are still appropriate today.

THE ESSENTIAL MISSION

VI

USING KNOWLEDGE WISELY

ONE POINT EMERGES with stark clarity from all we have said: higher learning and the nation's future are inextricably bound together. A new generation of Americans must be educated for life in an increasingly complex world. The quest for new knowledge must be intensified to unravel still further the mysteries that perplex us. And, through civic education, students of all ages must be prepared to participate more effectively in our social institutions. As these three goals are vigorously pursued, the nation's colleges and universities will fulfill, in new and vital ways, their traditional roles of teaching, research, and public service.

But higher learning has a still larger, more essential mission, one that concerns itself with the relationship of education to human conduct. Thirty-five years ago, the German philosopher, Karl Jaspers, identified the goal of education as *culture,* which he defined as "a given historical ideal [and] . . . a coherent system of associations, gestures, values, ways of putting things, and abilities." [1] The educated person, Jaspers concluded, was one to whom culture so defined had become second nature.

Yet today, a generation after Jaspers wrote, we find ourselves, as a nation, uncertain and deeply hesitant about higher education's larger social role. In Jaspers' terms, what *are* this society's agreed upon values and "ways of putting things"? For that matter, what, precisely, would characterize a person of culture, in Jaspers' sense, in our fragmented post-modern society? The absence of answers is haunting.

There was a time when colleges and universities felt no such uncertainties. They had the task of transmitting to the next generation, intact, society's moral, cultural, and political values and traditions. This mission was never truly achieved, and yet it was once so vital that in most nineteenth century colleges the presidents taught a "moral philosophy" course as the curricular capstone.[2] Even after the direct influence of the church declined, the conviction that the college represented a bastion of moral order was sustained; the afterglow of higher education's religious loyalty lingered.

But, as historian Henry May demonstrates so well in *The End of American Innocence*,[3] this confidence in the unity of the established order began to fade early in this century. The evaporation of Wilsonian idealism and the cultural upheavals of the 1920s hastened social fragmentation. Past certainties were shaken by scientific inquiry and higher education's confidence in its own moral mission weakened.

Still, for all the nagging doubts of the contemporary age, the belief persists that the process most capable of holding the intellectual center of society together, preventing it from disintegrating into unconnected splinters, is education. It may not have lived up to this vision of cohesion, but, at its best, the campus is expected to bring together the views and experiences of all its parts, and create something greater than the sum, offering the prospect that personal values will be clarified, and that the channels of our common life will be deepened and renewed.

A ringing call today for colleges and universities to concern themselves with values and society's concerns seems, at first blush, almost ludicrously quixotic. Not only is the cultural coherence of an earlier day gone forever, but the very notion of cohesion seems strikingly inapplicable to the vigorous diversity of contemporary life. Within the academy itself, subject specialties seem increasingly fragmented, splintered into innumerable functions. Robert Hutchins once described the modern university as a series of separate departments held together by a central heating system;[4] Clark Kerr has characterized it as an assemblage of faculty entrepreneurs held together by a common grievance over parking.[5]

There are even those who argue that the college classroom and the campus are rapidly becoming obsolete. They say that new teaching institutions are emerging that will carry on the work historically assigned to higher education.

Business and industry now offers courses ranging from basic skills instruction to postdoctoral seminars in science and mathematics. Impressive "corporate campuses" are cropping up across the country. Young people now spend more time in front of television sets than in the classroom. Satellites, computers, calculators, cable television, and videocassettes are the exciting new teachers of our time.

Higher education would ignore these developments at its peril. Job-based education offers students prospects for employment and promotion, and some businesses now confer accredited degrees. Someday soon, through new technology, almost any subject may be studied conveniently at home, and newspaper subscribers may routinely be able to "call up" on their home consoles stories from the pages of their favorite journals.

The crucial question is this: will the nation's colleges and universities offer something more than will be available to students in the corporate classroom or on videocassette? If so, how is it to be defined.

The nontraditional teachers have an essential role, offering information, training, and entertainment to all ages at convenient times, and in compelling ways. Still, we conclude that these new teachers are not likely to achieve the kind of understanding and wisdom that can result when students and teachers come together to gather data, test ideas, reflect upon deeper meanings, and weigh alternative conclusions. Through such encounters, information can be placed in larger context and the relationship of knowledge to life's dilemmas can be thoughtfully explored. These remain the special capacities of the classroom and the campus.

The danger is that, in a desperate bid for survival, higher education will imitate its rivals. If that happens, higher learning may discover that, having abandoned its special mission, it will find itself in a contest it cannot win. At a time when society's values are shaped and revised by the fashion of the marketplace, higher education's influence must grow outward from a core of integrity and confidence firmly rooted in humane goals that are currently lacking in most other institutions. This cannot happen if campuses turn themselves into educational supermarkets with a view toward mere fiscal survival.

Survival without a sense of mission is hardly preferable to extinction; indeed, it may be the forerunner of extinction. The ultimate loser would be a society that can no longer count on the cement that keeps it from falling apart, with people scattered into myriad unrelated cells, trained but not educated, sure of individuals' special desires and interests, but ignorant of shared purposes and ideals.

Education, by its very nature, is value-laden. Any institution committed to inquiry into the human experience must inevitably confront questions of purpose and meaning. The refusal to face those issues openly and directly is, itself, a moral decision with far-reaching implications. The late Jacob Bronowski, in a vivid description of his 1945 visit to Nagasaki harbor, raised deeply unsettling questions about education's response to humanity's most profound concerns.

What I had thought to be broken rocks was a concrete power house with its roof punched in. I could make out the outline of two crumpled gasometers; there was a coal furnace festooned with service poles; otherwise nothing but cockeyed telephone poles and loops of wire in a bare waste of ashes. I had blundered into this desolate landscape as instantly as one might walk among the craters of the moon. The moment of recognition when I realized I was already in Nagasaki is present to me as I write, as vividly as when I lived it. I can see the warm night and the meaningless shapes; I can even remember the tune that was coming from the ship. It was a dance tune which had been popular in 1945, and it was called "Is You Is or Is You Ain't Ma Baby?"[6]

For Bronowski, the lyrics of the dance tune took on macabre overtones. It was, he felt, a "universal moment," one in which modern man's knowledge was transformed into horror. At that instant of confrontation, he later wrote, "each of us in his own way learned that his imagination had been dwarfed."[7]

Hiroshima and Nagasaki—not to mention Dachau, Buchenwald, and Auschwitz—may, from one perspective, be irrelevant to the educational issues we confront today. Still, they have the odd effect of forcing us to inquire once again into deeply troubling, and perhaps unanswerable, questions about knowledge and its uses, about the relationship between education and human conduct. The destruction Bronowski witnessed was a technological achievement built on trained intelligence, and we cannot help wondering what discipline of mind, what knowledge more adequately comprehended, what values more effectively conveyed could have an equally powerful impact for human betterment?

"The deepest threat to the integrity of any community," writes John Gardner, "is an incapacity on the part of the citizens to lend themselves to any worthy common purposes." Gardner goes on to reflect on "the barrenness of a life that encompasses nothing beyond the self."[8] In response to such barrenness, America's colleges and universities need an inner compass of their own. They must perform for society an *integrative* function, seeking appropriate responses to life's most enduring questions, concerning themselves not just with information and knowledge, but with wisdom.

In the end, education's primary mission is to develop within each student the capacity to judge wisely in matters of life and conduct. This imperative does not replace the need for rigorous study in the disciplines, but neither must specialization become an excuse to suspend judgment or interfere with the search for worthwhile goals.

This is not to suggest a program of indoctrination in place of investigation; it is not a prescription for a rigid code of conduct for all students. We need no cultural or moral bandmasters striking up the tune to which everyone must dance. Indeed, we view with grave concern the growth of censorship and repression and the crusades of righteous zealots who seek to impose on others their own brand of morality. To counter such narrow and reactionary thinking, colleges should not push for particular conclusions; rather they should create a climate in which the values of the individual and the ethical and moral choices confronting society can be thoughtfully examined.

The aim is not *only* to prepare the young for productive careers, but to enable them to live lives of dignity and purpose; not *only* to generate new knowledge, but to channel that knowledge to humane ends; not *merely* to increase participation at the polls, but to help shape a citizenry that can weigh decisions wisely and more effectively promote the public good.

This is an awesome agenda. It calls for more than pious statements in catalogues, "op-ed" essays by college presidents, and exhortations at commencement time. What is needed is a carefully crafted general education program for all students that focuses on those experiences that integrate individuals into a community. In such a program, students should explore how their own society's values have been shaped, how they are enforced, and how societies react to unpopular ideas. Students should identify the premises inherent in their own beliefs and engage in a frank and searching discussion of ethical and moral choices.

Students also should confront the ethical implications of their chosen professions. In law, business, economics, and medicine, as well as in the sciences and arts, ethical issues arise every day. When does advertising edge over into deception and dishonesty? How does a physician determine the limits on his or her ability to save lives, and what does one do when that limit is reached? How should data be gathered, interpreted, and reported? What social concerns should influence the work of the architect, the geneticist, the industrial chemist, the newspaper reporter, the mining engineer? How can those in government reconcile private values and public expectations.

Finally, to act as a moral force in society, colleges and universities must confront more openly the ethical implications of their own procedures. We are troubled because, on many campuses, ethical corners are being cut. A 1979 Carnegie report cited a distressing array of questionable and misleading practices—deceptive advertising, poor academic programming, careless admissions, and financial aid procedures. If colleges expect to promote ethical behavior among their students, they must establish and maintain high ethical standards of their own.

American higher education has never been a static institution. For more than 350 years, it has shaped its program in response to the changing social context. As we look to a world whose contours remain obscure, the time has come for higher learning to adjust, once again, its traditional roles of teaching, research, and service. In so doing, it should affirm that at the heart of the academic enterprise there is something more than the heating system or the common grievance over parking.

The center holds because the search for truth leads to the discovery of larger meanings that can be applied with integrity to life's decisions. This, we conclude, is higher learning's most essential mission in the nation's service.

NOTES

NOTES

I. THE LOSS OF CONFIDENCE

1. Arnold, Matthew. *Poetry and Criticism of Matthew Arnold,* in A. Dwight Culler (ed.). (Boston, Houghton Mifflin, 1961).

II. A TRADITION OF SERVICE

1. Quoted in Cremin, Lawrence A. *American Education: The National Experience 1783–1876* (New York, Harper & Row, 1980) p. 116.
2. Rudolph, Frederick. *The American College and University: A History* (New York, Alfred A. Knopf, 1962) pp. 48–49.
3. Ibid., p. 229.
4. Ibid., p. 231.
5. Ibid., p. 238.
6. Ibid., p. 65.
7. Cremin, *American Education: The National Experience 1783–1876,* p. 516.
8. Cather, Willa. *My Antonia* (Boston, Houghton Mifflin, 1954) p. 258.
9. Quoted in Veysey, Laurence R. *The Emergence of the American University* (Chicago, The University of Chicago Press, 1965) p. 63.
10. Wilson, Woodrow. "Princeton in the Nation's Service," *Forum,* December, 1896, as reprinted in Hofstadter, Richard and Wilson Smith (eds.). *American Higher Education: A Documentary History* (Chicago, University of Chicago Press, 1961) p. 692.
11. Ibid., p. 689.
12. Steffens, Lincoln. "Sending a State to College," *American Magazine,* February 1909, reprinted in Stone, James C. and Donald P. DeNevi (eds.). *Portraits of the American University 1890–1910* (San Francisco, Jossey-Bass, 1971) p. 133.

13. Bush, Vannevar. *Science—The Endless Frontier* (Washington, National Science Foundation, reprinted 1980) pp. 10, 11.

14. U.S. National Center for Education Statistics, *Digest of Educational Statistics,* 1970, 1980.

15. Ibid.

16. U.S. Bureau of the Census. *Current Population Reports,* series P-20, No. 190, 1969.

III. EDUCATING A NEW GENERATION

1. Carnegie Council on Policy Studies in Higher Education. *Three Thousand Futures* (San Francisco, Jossey-Bass, 1980) p. 153.

2. Data compiled by The Carnegie Foundation for the Advancement of Teaching from information provided by the school systems mentioned, May 1981.

3. Special tabulations by The Carnegie Foundation for the Advancement of Teaching using Current Population Survey data for 1979.

4. Myrdal, Gunnar. "Future University" in Stroup, Thomas B. (ed.) *The University in the American Future* (Lexington, Ky., University of Kentucky Press, 1965) p. 101.

5. Bowen, Howard. *Educational Possibilities for Our Grandchildren* (Forthcoming) Ms. p. A-5.

6. Howard, H. Philip and Debra B. Rothstein. "Up, Up, Up, and Away: Trends in Computer Occupations," *Occupation Outlook Quarterly,* vol. 25, no. 2, Summer, 1981, p. 5.

7. Rimland, Bernard. "The Manpower Quality Decline: An Ecological Perspective" NPRDC TN 81–4 (San Diego, Navy Personnel Research & Development Center, November 1980) p. 12.

8. Ibid.

9. Quoted in Fuess, Claude M. *The College Board: Its First Fifty Years* (New York, Columbia University Press, 1950) p. 15.

10. Flexner, Abraham. *The American College* (New York, Century Co., 1908) p. 60.

11. Harvard Committee. *General Education in a Free Society* (Cambridge, Harvard University Press, 1945).

12. Agee, James, and Walker Evans. *Let Us Now Praise Famous Men* (Boston, Houghton Mifflin, 1960) p. 289.

1. Dupree, A. Hunter. *Science in the Federal Government* (Cambridge, Mass., Harvard University Press, 1957) pp. 27–29.

2. Calculated from *The World Almanac and Book of Facts 1981* (New York, Newspaper Enterprise Association, Inc., 1980) pp. 391–393.

3. National Science Board. *Science Indicators—1978* (Washington, National Science Foundation, 1979) pp. 15–16.

4. Ibid., p. 165.

5. Wolfle, Dael. "Forces Affecting the Research Role of Universities" in Smith, Bruce L. and Joseph J. Karlesky (eds.) *The State of Academic Science,* vol. 2. Background papers (New Rochelle, N.Y., Change Magazine Press, 1978) p. 39.

6. Thomas, L. "On the Uncertainty of Science," *Harvard Magazine,* vol. 83, no. 1, September–October 1980, pp. 19, 20.

7. Council on Environmental Quality and United States Department of State. *Global Future: Time to Act* (Washington, Government Printing Office, January 1981, p. x).

8. National Science Foundation. *National Patterns of Science and Technology Resources, 1980* (Washington, National Science Foundation, 1981) Table 15, p. 34.

9. National Science Foundation, special tabulations, August 1981.

10. Information supplied by Public Affairs Office, National Science Foundation, August 1981.

11. Ibid.

12. The National Science Foundation. *National Patterns of Science and Technology Resources,* 1980, p. 25.

13. Information provided by the General Electric Public Affairs Office in Washington, D.C., September, 1981.

14. Welch, John F., Jr. and Reginald H. Jones. "Comments from the Chairman and the Chairman Elect," *General Electric Investor,* annual report issue, 1980, p. 5.

15. Bush, Vannevar. *Science—The Endless Frontier* (Washington, National Science Foundation, reprinted 1980) pp. 18, 19.

16. Testimony by Donald Kennedy, President of Stanford University, and on behalf of the University, the Association of American Universities, and the National Association of State Universities and Land Grant

Colleges, delivered June 8, 1981 to the U.S. House of Representatives Committee on Science and Technology Subcommittee on Investigations and Oversight, on "Commercializing University Biomedical Research: Ethical and Institutional Impacts."

17. Ibid.

V. ADVANCING CIVIC LEARNING

1. Jefferson, Thomas. *Jefferson's Letters* compiled by Whitman Willson, (Eau Claire, Wisconsin, E. M. Hale, 1940) pp. 338–39. From letter to William Charles Jarvis, September 28, 1820.

2. *Report on American Values in the 80's: The Impact of Belief,* Research Forecasters, Inc., Commissioned by Connecticut Mutual Life Insurance Company, 1981.

3. Cited in Levine, Arthur. *When Dreams and Heroes Died: A Portrait of Today's College Student* (San Francisco, Jossey-Bass, 1981) p. 12.

4. Ibid., p. 21.

5. Mondale, Clarence. "With Tocqueville in Mind," *Phi Kappa Phi Journal,* vol. 41, no. 2, Spring 1981, p. 30.

6. Ashby, Eric. *Adapting Universities to a Technological Society* (San Francisco, Jossey-Bass, 1974) p. 30.

7. U. S. Bureau of the Census. *Current Population Reports,* Series P–20, no. 272, 1974; series P–20, no. 360, 1981.

8. Cross, K. Patricia. *Adults as Learners* (San Francisco, Jossey-Bass, 1981) pp. 201–204.

9. Ibid.

10. Wilson, Woodrow. "Princeton in the Nation's Service," *Forum,* December 1896, as reprinted in Hofstadter, Richard and Wilson Smith (eds.). *American Higher Education: A Documentary History* (Chicago, University of Chicago Press, 1961), p. 694.

VI. USING KNOWLEDGE WISELY

1. Jaspers, Karl. *The Idea of the University* translated by Reiche, H. A. T. and H. H. Vanderschmidt (Boston, Beacon Press, 1959) p. 30.

2. Rudolph, Frederick. *The American College and University: A History* (New York, Alfred A. Knopf, 1962) pp. 140, 141.

3. May, Henry. *The End of Innocence* (New York, Oxford University Press, 1979).

4. Kerr, Clark. *The Uses of the University* (Cambridge, Harvard University Press, 1963) p. 20.

5. Ibid.

6. Bronowski, Jacob. *Science and Human Values* (New York, Harper and Row, 1956) p. 3.

7. Ibid.

8. Gardner, John W. *Morale* (New York, W. W. Norton, 1978) p. 75.

In each case, they find special new challenges. Colleges must not only teach, but they must also educate a generation of students quite different from those of the past. Not only must they conduct research, but they must do so with reduced federal support and must consider enticing but potentially compromising allegiances with the private sector in our society. As a new approach to service, the authors advocate public policy studies for all students, especially encouraging a new program of civic education for adults. Then, as a capstone, they urge colleges and universities to help students and teachers alike use knowledge wisely so that higher education's dual role as servant and critic of society may be protected and advanced.

THE AUTHORS

Ernest L. Boyer is currently president of The Carnegie Foundation for the Advancement of Teaching. Formerly, he was U.S. Commissioner of Education.
Fred M. Hechinger is president of the New York Times Company Foundation.

THE CARNEGIE FOUNDATION
FOR THE ADVANCEMENT OF TEACHING
1785 Massachusetts Avenue, N.W.
Washington, D.C. 20036.
ISBN 0-91050-20-0 $6.50